Rebecca Thomas is a Welsh author and mother who bases her work on the cheeky charming world she sees around her.

With a passion to make her children smile, she writes everything with them in mind, driven by what they would like to read and listen to.

Princesses Wear Pants

REBECCA THOMAS

AUSTIN MACAULEY PUBLISHERS™
LONDON • CAMBRIDGE • NEW YORK • SHARJAH

A CIP catalogue record for this title is available from the British Library.

ISBN 9781398488984 (Paperback)
ISBN 9781398488991 (ePub e-book)

www.austinmacauley.com

First Published 2023
Austin Macauley Publishers Ltd
25 Canada Square
Canary Wharf
London
E14 5LQ

This book is dedicated to my beautiful girls. Thank you for being perfectly you.

My mum told me and now I am telling you,

There are some things princesses must always do.

Now you can brush your teeth, and I have
seen you comb your hair,
But there is always something lacking when you
go up the stair.

Zzz

I don't mind a muddy face, and I quite like
you in a tree,
But there is something cheeky that we
simply shouldn't see.

Phew!!

When your father has guests, or your sister has friends,

It's simply not the right sort of message we should send.

Especially at dinner, when Grandma comes to tea,

First course should be served with a

bit more dignity.

You are my girl, and I love you a lot,

But how many times do I ask, "Is there something you forgot?"

You do remember your manners and always
look so cute,
But it's always forgotten when you streak past
in your little birthday suit.

Or when you come home from school with a small graze on your knee,

I bend down and kiss it better and suddenly can't help but see.

You will be a strong, confident thing to behold,

But you really must be told.

PRINCESSES WEAR PANTS!

It's not enough just to remember your 'please' and 'thanks'.

Pop them on and you'll be fine...

But either way, I'm proud you're mine.

The End

Ingram Content Group UK Ltd.
Milton Keynes UK
UKHW020921110623
423187UK00008B/137

9 781398 488984